DROPS OF JOY

DROPS OF JOY

Copyright © 2012 by Moshe Shklar   **All rights reserved**

No part of this book may be used or reproduced in any manner whatsoever without written permission except in case of brief quotation embodied in critical articles and reviews.

Red Frog Publishing

redfrogpublishing@gmail.com

www.redfrogpublishing.com

112 Harvard Ave. # 43 Claremont, CA 91711.

Red Frog Publishing is a division of Red Frog Media

www.redfrogmedia.com

POETRY

1   2   3   4   5   6   7   8   9   10

ISBN-13: 0-9850276-0-6   ISBN-10: 0985027606

Book design by Starling

I would like to express my deep gratitude to poet William Willis, Prof. Marvin Zuckerman, Hershl Hartman and Miriam Coral for translating my Yiddish poems into English, and to my wife Dorothy and son Jerry for inspiring me to collect all these poems and bringing them to the readers. In this small collection are also included a few translations which were done by myself. Special thanks to my granddaughter Dina Szklarek for the editing.

Moshe Shklar

Drops of Joy

poems

by

Moshe Shklar

Translated from Yiddish

SHALOM

A singing, friendly shalom
Greeted me from all around
Flooded over my pounding heart,
Washed all the old bridges away.
Shalom! Cried out the earth's dry cracks,
Longing for rain,
Shalom! Cried out the shacks
Along the roads,
Shalom! Cried the rocks of the open field
Scattered to extremes without yield.

As I wandered about, a man
Neither stranger nor at home
In this land,
I moved between truth and dream,
Whispering through the deep silence,
Sholem, Sholem, Sholem!

A BISELE*

A *Bisele,* she said to me, with charm,
My grandmother spoke only Yiddish,
And my mother, too,
A *Bisele.*
So is it any wonder
That her Yiddish
With its Polish color
Caressed my ear
Like tender velvet
And perhaps even more,
A little...

_____
* A little

At least a *Bisele*,
And from that *Bisele*
More can emerge -
A full bowl.
Like my grandma
Who spoke only Yiddish
Used to say.
So, it's good to hear
In the *Bisele*
Of the youthful women
My grandmother's voice,
And my mother's,
And be delighted
Just a *Bisele*.

YOU DIDN'T KNOW

I spoke to you in Yiddish
And you pretended that you don't understand...
For you looked surprised
As if I was not of your world,

But from another time, from yesterday
Disappeared in smoke and flames.
You didn't know that I'm the keeper
Of my mother tongue.

You didn't know – without that tongue
I'm like an extinguished light,
You didn't know,
Or pretended that you didn't.

THE LAMENTING HANDS OF MY MOTHER

I see them always, everywhere.
They wring together in pain.
Two candles, a table, a prayer book,
Next to the hands of my mother.

The lamenting hands of my mother
At the threshold of the open door,
Two pale, tremulous flames

Follow after me in my footsteps.

They approach me from afar
And hover around my steps;
The flames cry out in my pathway,
Watch out, my son, watch out!

Oh, Mother, I'll watch out, I'll be careful
Of my life on its ruined stem –
I see candles, a table and in the middle
Burn the hands of my mother.

WHEN IT FALLS, AND WHERE IT FALLS

And suddenly it disappeared
The joy of sunrise and of blooming.
A darkness obscured my memory,
Where in the cells ashes still glow.

Again all around it is gray and cloudy,
From the sky bloody drops fall
On a child lying on the sidewalk
And the mother – a pillow for the child's head.

The horrific images are still with me
I thought they were gone forever,
But from the darkness they come
And open all old wounds again,

And it hurts each blood drop falling
And when it falls, and where it falls it hurts,
And the horrific images were never old,
Not at sunrise, not at sunset.

THE MOST BEAUTIFUL POEM

When I close the classroom door,
    As if out of torrent,
All the childish faces
That are no longer here,
That were drowned
In a vicious hour -
Emerged.

My hands and feet trembled
My throat was choked with tears,
Around me sat living remnants of my people -
Jewish children
Transformed
Into a silent audience.

The teacher introduced me
And asked,
"Please read a few of your poems…"
I read,
But it seemed to me
As if I descended
Into a deep valley
And could no longer hear
My own voice.

It is quiet in the classroom,
The quiet almost hurts,
And outside –
It is May.
A blooming tree
Peers into the room,
As if it wants
To ease
This very quiet.

And then,
A boy in the first row
Raises his hand:
"Friend poet,
Read the most beautiful poem..."
The most beautiful poem?
Which poem I should honor thus?
I leaf through all my verses
In my mind –
They are all equal,
Nurtured with pain and love.
So I stand there
               And look at a loss
At the chairs.
Finally
I decide:
The most beautiful poem,
                       My child,
Is the Yiddish tongue
In your mouth.

Remember!

AND LIVE WITH THEM

Almighty,
When I'll come to you with all my fortune –
A bunch of poems –
Don't make me feel ashamed,
Don't ask me with an ironic smile,
The way some are asking here
(Although poetry was always strange to them),

"What kind of language is it?
The letters look alike,
But the sound of the words
Died long ago in your world
And haven't reached me here in heaven."

I'm afraid you won't tolerate
My answer,
So I'll be silent
And stay on this earth
With the poems of my mother tongue,
And live with them, and live.

REMEMBER

Do you remember the wind's caress,
When the horizon was a fiery sunset?
Remember the words not said
That hung heavy on the branches
In a still deep silence?
Remember the snow that fell
And covered our shadow,
Which rose up again
To embrace us,
Make us stay together?

Remember the spring rain
When all ways lay open to us –
To our troubles and joys
And the endless hopes
That ran out in front of us?
Remember the wonderful rainbow
That blinded our eyes, then
Like a bird, flew away
And shrunk into the emptiness
Between lightning and thunder?

Remember the tree standing here,
Where I couldn't cry out my anguish?
But how should I remember it?
Like the tree you are gone
And only my longing remains.

HOW MANY POEMS

How many poems have I silenced
In the screaming days?
How many have remained lying
Like stones on the ground?

How many poems have I surrendered in pain
As I struggled with them?
Now, when fruits are ripening
I am left with them again.

MEAL-TIME

The wine weeps into the goblets
That are arranged around the edge of the table
Like the stars of Ursa Major
Without a head.

Four...

The ancestral goblets sparkle
In the evening light
And extinguish slowly
On the lips of the guests – my murdered brothers.

THE LITTLE DRESS FROM AUSCHWITZ

There was a little girl,
A little girl,
A little dress,
Just a little girl.

Her name was
Aidele
Unassuming, shy
But wise as she was small.

Everything she knew,
Loved delights,
A laugh, a chat,
A mischievous girl.

MOSHE SZKLAR

Her little tongue,
It twittered,
Her voice – a little bell ,
Her little eyes –
Two birdies,
That flew around, round All.

And so it was
Until
There came an evil man,
Screaming drunken and in laughter
Took away our Aidele,
The little girl,
The little dress,
The clever little one.

Drove her somewhere far away,
Where death itself did spread,
' Twixt barbed wire,
And brutal screams
Shneller, shneller, raus!

Lost from little Aidele,
The pretty little dress,
The little shoes,
The little scarf
From her clever head.

Driven in was Aidele,
Along with other little ones
Barefoot and naked
Into a white house.

There the dead already burned
And swallowed up the little girls,
The smoke just floated out.

There remained from little Aidele
The pretty blue dress,
A little dress,
A little girl,
A little dress-
Nothing more.

In Auschwitz lies the little dress,
Among the little shoes,
Little scarves,
In the very front.
There lies the little blue dress,
A little dress,
A little girl,
They call still for vengeance!

I DREAM OF THE CHILDREN

Dear little children,
Children so rare,
I see you again now,
Naked and bare.

And your little eyes,
So dark and so frightened
Tiny little birds
That call and entice me.

You be a bird too,
Come let us fly
From our twigs
To early morning highs

That there, in the ghetto,
Were consumed by fire.
Perhaps a mother may be there,
As we may aspire.

Perhaps we will find
In our roam
The vanished thresholds
Of our homes.

And the children go —
Through streets far-off yet.
Their little feet battered,
Their faces wet.

From sweat or from tears?
From blood or from rain?
They go on and their number
Grows greater again.

They go on and burst
Through fences near home.
And here is the Vistula
With waves spewing foam.

Will the river rinse off
The determined tread above,
Of little hearts yearning
For a mother's tender love?

They go and don't look
Back at what is behind.
The trees bow their heads
At the tread that they find,

And accompany the children
With tears that grow lighter.
The sun wonders at them
And shines even brighter.

And the water, which earlier
Was clear to the stream bed,
Now starts to seethe,
Glows red and more red.

In the glow of the redness
The tread falls and twists.
It leaves only deadness
And I – in its midst.

A TREE IN THE GHETTO

The tree broke off its hands – its branches,
Disheveled its golden leaves – its hair.
And I harken as it weeps in fearsome silence
For those cut off in youth, my peers.

It whispers its prayer to heaven and earth
As resin-tears drip upon its trunk.
Then in the twilight stillness it observes
A hellish flame with outstretched tongues

That guzzle the blood from the soiled concrete
Gingerly swallowing street after street,
But a grizzled elder is drawing near
Eyes afire with pain and hate.

He walks, and the wind kicks up his coat –
Broken wings that tumble down,
From afar chase after him choked howls
And hover around his head unbowed.

Soon he'll enter the sea of fire
And himself become a coal ablaze.
But see, he leaps over the fence of fire
The gaping horror left in his wake.

His gate is ever more youthful too,
Held aloft by his garment's wings;
As if the flame had birthed him anew,
From afar he appears but a child.

On and on he goes – and never fades –
Suspended on the horizon like a stain,
With earth and sky forever joined –
Shining like a torch with warnings and claims.

The tree broke off its hands – its branches,
Disheveled its golden leaves – its hair.
And it harken as it weeps in fearsome silence
For those cut off in youth, my peers.

CHAGALL'S STAINED GLASS WINDOWS

I don't know how
Your old town,
Vitebsk, looks today,
Chagall,
Your town
That I left
Many years ago
Among horrible explosions
Of fire and steel
In the inferno of war,
But as I stepped down
Into *Hadassah's* vestibule
In the new synagogue,
Embellished with your stained-glass windows,

I felt I had passed over a small bridge
And as in a mirage,
My memory began to fill
With pictures of the past.

*

Far in the past, so far...
Like the voice which guided
The twelve tribes
Over Jordan's surface,
I'm guiding my sight
Split into halves
By blue and red colors,
And hang it on
A stain of green, inflamed
By the sun penetrating from outside.
At once all the herdsmen,
The sons
Of the ancient tribes disappeared
And only a goat was left alone,
My well-known goat
Quietly nibbling on the straw
From Vitebsk's low roofs
In search of her stable.
Whose fate have you entrusted her,
Chagall?

*

The past, the past…
I hear my mother's voice
See her screaming hands
Stretching out from the fire,
Shaking the new synagogue,
Shattering its walls.

From the windows
The tribe of Judah descends
And marches towards me –
They fill the roads
Marching with past generations.
Of those disappeared into flames
From ghettos,
           Crematories,
                      And pogroms.
They are passing through an abyss
Like the red sea in the Torah.

Now it all ceases…
I awake
In the small vestibule
And again I'm among
The stained glass you cut,
Marc Chagall.

THE LAST CUP

The last cup is not yet drained,
The last word has not been lost,
Somewhere embers still reflect sounds
And warm shards of goblets.

We look at them – our yesterdays,
With brown-blue scars on our soul,
Which flutter in between days and nights,
As if they have fallen into an abyss.

We try to take them out,
And piece them together with burning fingers,
But they disintegrate again
Only the sleepless nights hear their echoing.

So, it is our fate to collect the shards
Of a murdered generation,
But they will stay sacred
In our rippling memory to the last cup.

I AM THE TEAR

I am the mushroom cloud above Hiroshima,
I am the ashes of the Warsaw Ghetto
I am the voice of millions
Lost in the echo of eternity,
Taken away to the farthest
Unknown, where time ceases.
I am the scorched earth of Vietnam,
And in Ponary the earth was pulled over me.
I am a mother's tear in the camp,
And also her child on an electric fence.
I am the child's scream never heard,
The words burned up with their bodies.

I am the father from Tel-Aviv
Who mourns his son at Sinai.
I am the son who could not find
His father's grave on the battle field.
I am lost in space, drifting
In my torn clothes of mourning.

I am a the child of Sarajevo
With bald eyes of fear.
I am the black cloud of Auschwitz
Which heaven covered over,
Yet it still hangs there above us
In the air – the sign of Cain.

MY CITY IS ON FIRE

The smoke reaches the sky,
Black curling smoke.
Crimson fire-flames dive
And tear around the edges
Of walls and roofs,
And with the flooding air
From the earth
The black curls of smoke
Dance higher and higher,

All at once, I know
I have seen such flames before,
It was when they sought out
The hiding children along
With the other ghetto folk –
The cinders choke me
But I'm not yet ready to take
My last breath on foreign soil.

How start again such fires,
Here in the city of angels?
Can the fire heal wounds
Made by raging time?
Oh, put out those angry flames!
The city is still so beautiful.
Let her become our mother,
A mother for you and me.

    *

Still
The sky is finally clear
Above my city,
A burned out satchel
Gathering up ashes.
Her faces
Not yet masked
From the wounds
That will heal up
Into a cracked smile.

She is coming to herself
My city
Like the lonely angel
That escorts one
To the city of graves.
And now she stands
Lost.
Oh, what is happening to you
City of angels
Who is running away
With the flames?

KINNERET

In the still hour of dusk
The sky hangs calm and blue
Over *Kinneret*, the sea.
From hills shadows fall to the depths,
In the still hour of dusk
And douse the sunny flame.

Fishermen approach the shore,
A day's labor is done –
Now they unload their haul.
On their faces the mark remains
Of the day's labor they've left behind
And the air fills with song.

MOSHE SZKLAR

From afar I have stumbled here
And my hearing I now make sharp –
The sound cuts deep into my heart:
Kinnert, Kinneret, Kinner...
How hard it is to part, how hard,
With this yearning song.

THE DAY FADES IN STILLNESS

In my world – the little garden –
The summer has already withered.
On narrow footpaths
The shadow of autumn falls
And distant rays –
Bands of gold
Tangle
At my feet
Silently,
Silently,
The day fades
And trembles
In between the fences.

SIERRA NEVADA

I would probably
Never have reached
The proud mountains
Of the Sierra Nevada
If I hadn't been
Chased away
By the mad winds
Of my native
Carpathian mountains,

And although a mild wind
Is blowing now at my back
And I'm ready to kneel
Before the sacred silence
Hanging here
In the air,
I'm still unable
To find peace.

I imagine that I see again
"Babia Gora"*, which
Suddenly becomes
"Babi Yar"** and
Swallows me
Together with the Sierra.

---

* *"Babia Gora"* is a summit in the Polish Carpathian Mountains.

** *"Babi Ya*r*"* is a valley in the vicinity of Kiev in the Ukraine, where the Nazis murdered over a hundred thousand Jews.

DROPS OF JOY

The night did not bestow its calm
The ocean grew more stormy still
And waves beat steadily upon the shore;
The sound like deafening music's trill
That devastates my heart.

A lightning bolt, a bright, sharp knife,
Cut through the gloom and pall,
And, along with the thunder and the strife,
Stars began their brilliant fall
And disappeared into the sea.

Suddenly, the sea yawned wide,
And brilliant light poured upon the sea.
I searched for stars within its depths
And found – just me.

*

Ere dawn the seas grew still
And ocean waves rocked peacefully within,
And as far as gaze can reach and see
The calmness rules... the calm.

A mild blue haze envelops all,
The far off hills, the deepest vale.
And over all the sun arose
As yesterday, as days grown pale.

As if nothing here had happened by:
No stormy seas, no flames of fire,
And I could not my star espy,
Fallen in depths, there to expire.

*

The oar's still tightly groped
In the five-fingered vise at the prow
And drops of sweat, like drops of joy,
Stand upon my graying brow.

There are strengths still left to me
But who can tell how long they'll last?
Then lead me, boat, through stormy sea;
There's still much time till all is past,

Until I get to heaven's blue –
That swoops away and rushes toward –
I hardly know just what to do,
But moving on is its own reward.

*

And I would join the dance right here,
While the beat of wind and sound are strong
But it's not my music, not my sound I hear,
It's not my song.

Electronic music's sound
Drowns out, I think, its own voice, too.
I can't hear anything, I've found
Only my eyes take in the view

Of swirling feet and hands and feet
That carries back my reeling mind
To music of another kind
That once inspired a burning beat.

I carry them about with
The lyrics of that remembered song:
"Darling, see –
Take my hand and come with me!"

And she extends her willing hand,
And I approach with blinded eye,
But in our path a firewall stands:
She fades away, as smoke in sky.
The music roars, and the ocean's spray
That carries me back to yesterday.

FOR AS LONG AS A YIDDISH POEM RESOUNDS

For Peretz Markish

Come all into the funeral march
Unto the secret grave,
Where still the Yiddish poem endures,
And bursts itself from out his breast,
Just as, through all his life,
It bursts out of his pen,
And with its steering sound,
Tears open the deepest dark.

So what if you find the road is hard
That you are weary of it?
But put your ear close to the earth,
As his friend has bid you,
And listen: there poems gurgle.
Like a stream, surging and undammed
His " Brothers" rage on
Against the aged world.
And once again the old woodcarver goes
With pious prayers upon his lips
Ready to spill the hangman's blood,
And crack his ribs,
And to greet the drowning morrow
With brightness and with love,
And to cleanse with light the earth
Of pain and lonely sorrow.

Somewhere still, on distant roads,
His coat hems thrown askew,
Mantses seeks a reckoning
From him whose name
Was paired with steel –
A reckoning for choked-down words
Thrown into the abyss

And, yet, still heard from there.
As a fresh breeze among branches
His poems sound and stir.
And they will never cease from sounding,
Stirring up the weary.
Hear – his poems still sing on,
As does our poet-victim.

THE FINAL SONG

They would have reached a hero's age by now,
And many works of aged seers,
But for the red flooded undertow...
It seems to me, I hear, I hear
Markish'es and Fefer's call,
Enmeshed in rifle-fire's coils –
A tightened noose around it all.
But, like a swallow, it tears loose from its toils
And flies up high through space and time's infinity
To eternity.

And the final song peals forth
In the angelic words of Bergelson and Hofshteyn,
Der Nister, Kvitko, all the rest
Who paid with blood and pain
For their faith and for their zest,
Of the Jew.

They would have reached a hero's age by now
Had murder not destroyed.
But see, the light endows
Their words, heroically deployed
Across length, breadth, depth, and all endeavor
For us – the people – and forever!

YOUNG CLEZMORIM, OLD NIGUNIM

Young *clezmorim*, old *nigunim* –
The fiddle, the bass and the flute
Lighten up the hall and the light
Takes me away back in time.

Tunes are mixing quiet sounds
With happy blow from drum...
Hey, *clezmers,* where are you riding,
Disappearing from my sight?

Who is Berl and who is Yiddl
Who is moving the bow and who plays flute?
Suddenly across me comes the fiddle alone
And Yiddl isn't anymore there.

The bass – a beard without fringes and face
Tears apart the night with his sigh,
I'm trying to see him,
Who brought him here close by?

It's not celebration, not a wedding,
Oy, brothers, where are you coming from?
The light is off, the table empty,
Only a *ningun* fluttered around.

TO MY TWO GRANDCHILDREN

THREE POEMS

ALL THE ANSWERS

And here we will stop,
My child,
Your questions hurt too much,
Wait a moment,
Wait a moment,
All the answers did dry out,
Like water
In a well,

And the deaf echo
Is carried away by the wind.
Maybe they'll return
With the under heart current
And the last answer,
My child
You'll find in my sight.

ONLY POETS

The house of white paper
Which you have built
With your fingers
Is shaking
Like your small world
And will soon
Crack, collapse,
I doubt if even Samson
Could support it.
Perhaps only poets
Could.

AS LONG

As long as my legs are wise enough –
Let's dance.
I'll dance and dance, I'll dance and laugh,
And watch the glitter in your eyes.

Who knows how long they'll carry me,
My heavy legs?
As long as they don't need a carriage,
Let's dance…

Dance till sundown on the clear sky,
Like your blue eyes,
And not notice when they'll become
Full with tears like dew.

And when I'll, like daylight, disappear,
And nothing will remain, of sort,
One thing remember please
My last unspoken words.

A BENCH IN THE GARDEN

Oh, how I lament
The bench in the garden!
How long has it been, how long
Since I played there
With your soft, tender hand
And lost a wager,
My hardened heart.

It stands empty now
In our garden.
The trees are sick
Of the long waiting.
Spring is still anticipating
Your arrival
And my friend, summer
Has prepared its lap.

Autumn spreads its leaves
Across the bench,
Its gold – a gift for your eyes,
Restless and anxious,
Winter has become harsher –
Oh, don't, I beg you, don't let
My heart expire.

WITHOUT YOU

How empty all around
Without you.
The trees stand silent
Without you.
A flower weeps in the window
Without you.

Night interrupts its journey
Without you.
Day grows gray and dull
Without you,
Because with all my heart I gaze
At you.

WHEN FLOWERS DIE

The flowers on the table
Are already withering
Like somebody has
Wiped out their colors.

Just yesterday you took them
From my hand with so much love
And pressed them against your heart
As if embracing me.

Now they are standing so sad,
My flowers and shrinking,
On the petals the dew
Is drying out, like tears.

I know, flowers too must die,
But I'm so sorry
For the withering colors,
And for your sight
Which hangs with sadness
On the flowers.

WITHOUT A WORD

Everything was told already
With a wink.
Now we are in silence counting
Every Spring.

How many have already past,
And how long
Will we, my love, continue
Our walk

To the blue which is so far –
Without an end,
To the light which could still
With its glare

Awake in our heart
The joy
Which could heal
Old wounds?

Oh, You didn't spare us,
No, my Lord,
So now we are just counting the Springs
Without a word.

AUTUMN

Grief, gray like a curtain
covers all windows
in the houses of my city
the sad doves coo -
in their eyes
the secret whirls
constant passings
and rebirths
quiet turns off the pale light of day
and streetlights
glow
like flowers.

WORDS

Words, words, words,
Empty words
Like sand on the shoreline
Wind, take them far away
And return to me the joy
of silence
between the two of us

I KNOW

I know
You will leave
With summer
Great sadness
Will hang
Over me
Through all autumn
Maybe longer
And again I am ready
For a moment of joy

All the sadness
Of the world
Worn
Like pearls of dew on a string
Which bring
Green serenity.
And you...?

IT'S SOLACE

Like a tree in the spring
I am coming back to you
Born again
With new songs.
But you constantly
Find in them
Old tunes
Which once
Caressed your ears
And then were scattered
Like autumn leaves
In the wind.

My child!
The tree is not getting younger
Though it is flourishing
And maybe there is some solace in knowing
That it is always changing.
It's still -
A stranger.

DROP OF LIGHT

Like Moses who forced
water from stone
I want to extract from my words
at least a shimmering drop
and carry it toward
unknown sunrises
ambushed in nooks
of remote eras
and separating existences.

And if my words
do not survive
then let this drop linger
as a small
flickering star
which can
change into a sun.

FAREWELL TO MY SISTER CHAYA

I couldn't even say Farewell,
You vanished, gone,
Leaving in my heart
Deep wounds
Without a cure.
I thought we could still
See each other sometimes
Recall the days
When we had to share
The pain
Like a loaf of bread

Piece by piece
On the scale of time
Measuring the happy moments
When spring brought into the house
The first rays
And the snow fell off the walls
Leaving wet black stains,
And you tried
With a rag,
Like with a magic wand
To cover them –
My big, little sister.

Oh, the black stains,
They stay with me
On all my wanderings
Through the world
And they recall
The days of frost
And snow storms,
And all the sufferings
Which you went through,
My big, little sister.
Now you are gone,
Vanished,
And nobody, nobody
Can heal my old wounds –
My big, little sister.

IN A POLISH YIDDISH SHTETL

In the Polish Yiddish *shtetl*
Minsk Mazovietzki
Where my mother and father
Came from
There was a tombstone
On the grave of my *zaide*
Fishl the tailor
That's all
That is left
Of the *shtetl's* Jews

Home-workers like him
Fishl the tailor
Common people and scholars
Peddlers and paupers...
A lonely tombstone
In the midst of an open field
Plowed
By wind and time
Looking at the world
With poked out eyes
Two Hebrew letters
Pay Nun *
Jewish wanderers
From all around
If you'll go there
And see the tombstone
You should know
Fishl the tailor
Was my *zaide*
A common Jew
Like all the *zaides*
With beard and side locks
And soft voice
With open eyes
To the skies.

In each garment he saw his heart
And with blessing
Let it out.
In my dreams I see
It's flying there
The last garment with the last prick
From the flushing needle
In his hand
And spreading
Like a black cloud over the blood stained
Polish soil

*

Can somebody tell me
If my *zaide's* tombstone
In the Polish Yiddish *shtetl*
Minsk Mazovietzki
Still exists?

* *Po Nitmar(Pay Nun):* Here is Hidden

WITH EYES CLOSED

With eyes closed
　　I'll see you anyway
And read you like pages
Of a book.
With eyes closed
I'll recognize you
Among a forest of trees
As the one tree
I searched for
My entire life.

With eyes closed
I'll approach you
Blind,
And not open my eyes
So that we both don't
Disappear.

AT CLOSE OF DAY

Swiftly comes the close of day
Like the gas lights that used to flicker
As day went out
On the street corner
Where I stood speechless
Searching for the stars.

Darkness took hold
Everywhere
And my childish heart trembled
In fear.

Shadows played
With shadows, teasingly
Chasing me here and there
Obscuring my way.

Since then I regret
When day comes to close at night
With darkness the thresholds assail.
I sicken and imagine
That the gas light still flickers.
And till the stars grow bright
I want to exclaim –
Let there be light, let there be light!

SHADOW-SHINE

To come upon the yearning
To return to that field
By the blue river
To that sunset
That glowed red
And swiftly slunk away
Leaving only blue shadows
To wander in the grass
Till night concealed utterly alone.
Nothing was forbidden

As on the eve of creation.
I felt entirely reborn
Ready to spring like a deer
And sing praises to the sky.
But like the sun
You slunk away
And of your shadow there remained
But a pale shine.

STAY

Throughout the night you appeared in my dream
And what didn't we converse about?
Reminisced about your street, your window up above,
The flowers on the iron balcony.
The tree that fluttered in the wind
And lulled you to sleep
The river in which we swam
In the cool end-of-summer eves
And that first moist touch of lips...
The entire world was envious of us
And we laughed at the world
In wanton hearty glee.

Throughout the night you appeared in my dream
And we talked and talked,
Unaware that dawn was about to break
As we were still in our exchange…
So much said, so much left unsaid,
And words, I think, sink in a well
And we along with them.
From the depths I stretch out my hand to you
And repeat as once in my song –
Stay, and at least for a moment be real!

WORD GLOW

For Rivka Basman Ben-Chaim

O, word glow,
From wisdom's essence...
A musical order
Unites them.
   Cyprian Kamil Norwid

The words that glow
With wisdom and woe,
Become song,
And sense in them one may
The heart's trembling,

The tree's sap,
The violin's still note
And the dream
Gone astray,
Sense in them one may
Fleeting luck
And the music
Of words that glow
With wisdom and woe
When they become
Song.

IF THERE NO MORE REMAINS

And if there no more remains anyone
To enjoy a book in Yiddish
Then poems like moonstones
Will only ornament museums

I won't yet despair
And my books I will send
To my long-time friends
Those friends whose eyes are veiled

MOSHE SZKLAR

Who came to me in dreams at night
And whom I can't forget,
To the friends in the valleys of the dead –
Nameless, with no address.

Yet they had so many books
Unread, untouched,
When the terrible whirlwind
Cast them into the ghettos.

So they must still read poems,
Those old friends of mine,
And if no one is left,
I'll start over again
To write poems for them.

IN THE WHO-KNOWS-WHERE

I'd like to send you, my friend
The loveliest gift –
All the pages of my new book
Bound in blood red
Like the poems that float about there
Between its leaves.
But you've vanished
In the blue distances,
In the who-knows-where
And I can't find you,
And I can't rest.

So I don't know
If it makes sense
To keep searching for your tracks
And be irked day and night
For not following
Your path.

Whether I send you my book
Or not, whether you sift through it,
As you once did my thoughts,
Together
We'll endure
And glimmer…

EVENING LIGHT

The day ends
In red flame
Hides itself in the sea
But somewhere
The evening light
Rocks as if on a scale
Soon it will also fade
Fade
I will remain standing there
And will wait, suspiciously –
What will the night bring?

TRACES

The days run toward the future
And are no more
But behind every day
Every hour
Somewhere
A trace is left
That is braided
Forever
Into eternity

And I seek in that trace
The meaning of yesterday

DON'T ASK

Ask not why
Sadness is black
Joy is green
And indifference
Has no colors
The answer
Of a Daltonist
Could easily mislead you

KEYS

In an old hardware store
I found some keys
That fit every door
So all about I go
Uninvited
And seek
Myself

But keys can also mislead
Even when they lead
Through all doors

MY YIDDISH SONG

*Upon hearing Eleanor Reissa
at the "Yiddishkayt" Festival*

Such a homey Yiddish,
my Warsaw Yiddish
coming from my parents,
my Yiddish song...
From streets and courts
my childhood's song
came a-running
annoying and shouting:

Harshl where ya goin',
Harshl where ya puttin'
yer beefy hands...

Oh, Harshl, where are you,
Oh, Harshl, where are you lying,
where are your remains?
Hands no more,
walls no more –
just a pile of stones
and stones hark back
to the Yiddish tune
in which one hears
an echo, the sound
of Yiddish songs
that wander about
and no one responds,
silence throughout.

Oh, Harshl, where are you,
Oh, Harshl, where are you lying,
Oh, Harshl, my Harshl,
make yourself known!
And Harshl isn't replying,
nor is Velvl, nor Berl,
nor Yankl, nor Shmerl –
just the weeping of the wind.

And in the windy howl
I hear their voices
coming from a distance,
from the distant past.

From those streets,
from those courts,
where children
in Yiddish cavorted,
where mamas fondly
enveloped them
and youngsters
in Yiddish courted.

Oh, Harshl, where are you,
Where is your house?
No more house,
no more court,
all is vanished
in smoke and dust...

Singer, sing your Yiddish song,
revive with your tune
a world that is gone!

CONTENTS

Shalom 7

A Bisele 9

You Didn't Know 11

The Lamenting Hands Of My Mother............................13

Translation by William Wallis

When It Falls And Where It Falls 15

Translation by M. S.

The Most Beautiful Poem 17

Translation by Marvin Zuckerman

And Live With Them 21

Translation by M. S.

Remember..23

Translation by A. Lenkawicki & W. Wallis

How Many Poems 25

Meal Time 27

Translation by Marvin Zuckerman

The Little Dress From Auschwitz ……………………………….29

    Translation by Michaela Safadi & Hershl Hartman

I Dream Of The Children………………………………………..…….33

    Translated by Hershl Hartman

A Tree In The Ghetto ……………………………………....…………..37

    Translation by Miriam Coral

Chagall's Stained Glass Window ………..…………………………..39

The Last Cup ……………………………………………………...………..43

I Am The Tear……………………………………………………….……...45

    Translation by A. Lenkawicki & W. Wallis

My City Is On Fire ……………………………………………………..…..47

    Translation by Ester Cohn & W. Wallis

Kineret ……………………………………………………………………….51

    Translation by Miriam Coral

The Day Fades In Stillness …………………………………………..53

    Translation by Marvin Zuckerman

Sierra Nevada ……………………………………………………….……..55

    Translation by M. S.

Drops Of Joy 57

For As Long As Yiddish Poem Resound 61

The Final Song 65

Translation by Hershl Hartman

Young Clezmorim, Old Nigunim 67

Three Poems..69

Translation by M. S.

A Bench In The Garden 73

Without You... 75

Translation by Miriam Coral

When Flowers Die 77

Without A Word 79

Translation by M. S.

Autumn..81

Words..83

I Know...85

It's Solace...87

Drop Of Light...89

Translation by ASF

Farewell To My Sister Chaya ……………………………………..91

In A Polish Yiddish Shtetl …………………………………………..93

Translation by M. S.

With Eyes Closed ………………………………………………………..97

At Close Of Day ………………………………………………………….99

Shadow-Shine ……………………………………………………………101

Stay ……………………………………………………………………………103

Word Glow…………………………………………………………………105

If There No More Remains …………………………………………..107

In The Who-Knows-Where……………………………………………109

Translation by Miriam Coral

Evening Lights ……………………………………………………………..111

Traces …………………………………………………………………………113

Don't Ask ……………………………………………………………………115

Keys ……………………………………………………………………………117

Translation by Marvin Zuckerman

My Yiddish Song …………………………………………………………119

Translation by Miriam Coral

www.ingramcontent.com/pod-product-compliance
Lightning Source LLC
LaVergne TN
LVHW011206080426
835508LV00007B/638